Holy Obsession

FROM THE BIBLE TEACHING MINISTRY OF
STEPHEN DAVEY

WISDOM FOR THE HEART

HOLY OBSESSION

Author: Stephen Davey
Editorial Team: Josh Wredberg and Karen Wredberg
Cover Design and Text Layout: Shannon Brown, Advanced Graphics (www.advancegraphics.us)
ISBN 978 0 9908050 4 5

Contents

Three Radical Refusals

Romans 15:14

One hundred seventy years ago in Scotland, there appeared briefly, a man considered by Christians worldwide today to be a shining light. His name was Robert Murray McCheyne.

McCheyne entered the pastorate in 1836, at the age of twenty-three. He would only serve for six years, dying in a typhus epidemic when he was twenty-nine. By that time, his passion for Christ had already made its mark. His commitment to holy living became almost legendary. His sermons and writings were heard and read throughout Scotland, and influenced untold thousands to give their lives in total surrender to Jesus Christ.

If you read of the life of Robert Murray McCheyne, you come away with the thought that this man was obsessed with the things of God. He was obsessed with the glory of God; obsessed with the preaching of the gospel; and obsessed with the grace of Christ.

McCheyne challenged believers to live a similar life; a life obsessed with godly priorities.

"Remember, you are God's sword, His instrument—a chosen vessel unto Him to bear His name. In great measure, according to the purity of the instrument, will be the success. It is not great talent that God blesses so much as great likeness to Jesus Christ. A holy [Christian] is an awesome weapon in the hand of God."[1]

If any words best described the heart and life of the apostle Paul, I think it could be the phrase, "holy obsession." Like Robert Murray McCheyne, Paul was obsessed with the glory of God, the gospel of God, and the grace of God, and he was always challenging the believer with their potential and purpose as an instrument in the hand of God.

In Romans chapter 15, the apostle makes a shift in his writing to inform us that he is now in the process of wrapping up his letter; which does not mean he is finished. He actually has a lot more to say. He is like most preachers who say, "Now, finally…," and you know they are nowhere near finality!

Do not think for a moment that Paul is finished teaching in this letter. In Romans 15:14, Paul does begin his closing comments, which are personal, passionate, and provocative.

And concerning you, my brethren, I myself am convinced that you yourselves are full of goodness, filled with all knowledge, and able also to admonish one another. (Romans 15:14)

Paul is commending them. It is a rare thing for Paul to write a letter without even one rebuke, yet the letter to the Romans arrives without a single reprimand.

This letter is so different from his letter to the Corinthians. He refers to them as immature babies, unable to receive even the most basic teaching of truth (1 Corinthians 3:1–2).

It is also different than the letter by the writer of Hebrews. He refers to his scattered audience as people who are poor listeners and slow learners (Hebrews 5:11–13).

Instead of these rebukes, Paul is able to entirely commend these believers who are living in Rome. He writes, "I am convinced you are people of…" character (full of goodness); conviction (filled with all knowledge); and competency (able to admonish one another).

Every believer who desires to be an awesome weapon in the hand of God will make three radical refusals.

- A person of good character is choosing not to be evil or bad.
- A person of conviction is choosing not to float down the stream of relativism.
- A person who is competent to admonish is choosing not to ignore other people.

For those who are truly obsessed with holy living, their life will say "no," as much as it says "yes." A holy life is as much a life of refusing the wrong things as it is a life of accepting the right things.

If there was ever a need for radical refusals to take place it was in the days of Paul—and it is in our generation, as well.

The Romans believers were living in what Seneca, the first century playwright, called "the cesspool of iniquity." This was a reference to the capitol city of the Roman Empire, where Paul was mailing this letter.

The immorality of Rome was almost beyond description. Everything from bisexuality to bestiality was applauded.

The highest political leader of Rome was a known pedophile. Abortion was commonplace. Unwanted children were left on doorsteps to be taken and eaten by wild animals or worse, if there can be something worse, by human predators who would raise these children and then, turn them out as child prostitutes. A man and a woman who married and remained faithful were mocked by the Roman philosophers as prudes and simpletons.

The religions of Paul's day worshiped a pantheon of gods as wicked and petty as human beings. Their chief god was in reality, the human body.

Drug abuse was so widespread that when Paul preached in Ephesus, the people gave up their mind-altering drugs.

If there was ever a day when people needed to learn how to refuse corruption, immorality, superstition, drug abuse, sexual promiscuity, drunkenness, and so on—it was then, and it is now.

The refusals of the believers in Rome need to be the radical refusals of every Christian today. If a Christian is to have these holy obsessions; that is, to be passionate, gripped, preoccupied, fixated, and fanatical over holy things, there must be radical refusals in order to see it happen.

Radically Refuse Mediocrity

To put this in a positive light—a Christian should be characterized by acts of goodness.

Notice again that first phrase Paul uses to describe these believers.

...I myself am convinced that you yourselves are full of goodness,... (Romans 15:14)

The original word translated "full of" is the same word that is used of a sponge when it is full of liquid. Whatever is in the sponge will come out when the sponge gets squeezed. Paul is saying, "When life squeezes you, what ought to come out is goodness."

It is interesting to me that the word for goodness in this verse is also given to us as one of the fruits of the Spirit of God. When the believer surrenders to the internal reforming work of the Holy Spirit, fruit emerges.

...the fruit of the Spirit is love, joy, peace, patience, kindness, and goodness,...(Galatians 5:22)

Since God is entirely, essentially, and absolutely good (Matthew 19:17), when we grow into the likeness of Christ, goodness squeezes out.

Goodness is the work of Christ in us through the Spirit of God. This means goodness is not something you drum up; it is not the result of self-effort. It is also not a New Year's resolution or a reward for attending church and never skipping Sunday School. Goodness is the process of reformation—it is the making of a holy heart.

Goodness is the result of an extreme makeover in which the Spirit of God bulldozes everything to the ground and starts from scratch as you surrender to Him.

People will say of a man or woman under reconstruction by the Spirit of God—"That is a good man," or "That is a good woman." It is becoming, more and more, a rare commendation of someone.

Many years ago, Mark Twain said, with a cynical grin on his face, "Always do the right thing. It will gratify some people and astonish everybody else."

The *Daily Herald* of Chicago, a couple of years ago, ran an article about a newlywed couple who lost all their money. This couple had left a black zippered case—the size of a personal calendar—on the roof of their car as they sped away from their reception to begin their honeymoon. The case had all their wedding gift money and other cash gifts from their parents zipped up tight inside. When they reached their destination, it was gone.

Two days after the newspaper ran the story, the same newspaper carried the headline, "Finders Keepers? Not Everyone Believes It." David Yi, an unemployed suburban resident, had found the black case with the $12,000 inside. In spite of the fact that he was unemployed and had mounting bills, he tracked down the couple and gave it back to them. After this hit the newsstands, David was inundated with job offers! With employee theft in the billions every year, it is easy to understand why he received so many.

The truth is, goodness is so rare that we are surprised when it happens and are not quite sure how to respond.

A *USA Today* poll found 1 out of every 2 employees admitting to some form of unethical or illegal activity. This might be cutting corners on quality control, covering up incidents, lying about sick days, or deceiving customers.

Justin Martyr, who lived in Galilee in the second century, made an interesting observation about Jesus Christ's work as a carpenter. You may remember that the Lord was a carpenter until the age of thirty, when he entered the ministry. Justin Martyr actually wrote about farmers still using plows and yokes for the oxen made by Jesus Christ—seventy-five years later!

Goodness is not necessarily discovered in church—it is demonstrated at work and in life. It is the refusal of mediocrity.

Track the word "goodness" or "good" through the New Testament sometime and feel the urgency of God to see his children demonstrate excellence in character, in occupation, in relationships, in all of life.

Earlier, Paul said we should,

…Abhor what is evil; cling to what is good. (Romans 12:9)

These are strong words. We are to despise sin and literally, glue ourselves to good.

Twice Paul challenges the believer to do what is good as a citizen of earth and heaven (Romans 13:13).

Paul gave a pep talk to the Galatians when he wrote,

Let us not lose heart in doing good… (Galatians 6:9a)

Doing good does not automatically result in thank you cards, notes of appreciation, a promotion, or a bonus at work. We can easily lose heart.

Perhaps you have felt the discouragement, and even resentment, when the lazy, conniving employee received "Employee of the Month." You are the one who has been sweating it out, faithfully taking on not only your tasks, but even helping that employee with his.

I learned firsthand the perils of working a little too hard while I was in college. Several of my friends and I worked on an assembly line, making microwave ovens. All I had to do on the assembly line was to attach two metal legs onto a small motor and then press a plastic fan onto the motor—a small internal fan used to cool the microwave. When I finished making it, I had to hand it over to the worker on the assembly line just a few feet away, and then start on another one. The guy who had been assigned this post before me had only a couple of them assembled and ready for the assembly line.

I was afraid it might be a difficult spot. However, after working for only three hours, I had boxes of the part stacked around me—ready and waiting. I pulled a box of them over to the line so that the guy only had to reach in and he was ready to go.

I thought, "This is too easy!"

It was so easy, in fact, that it became downright boring. What I did not realize was that the guy before me wanted the job to appear to be difficult, so he would not have to do anything else. He wanted to be bored; he lived to be bored.

I naively jumped onto the line to help anywhere I could. I discovered after a few days, that I was upsetting the people I was trying to help—I was disturbing the culture of mediocrity. One guy muttered under his breath to me, "What are you doing—trying to make everybody look bad?"

The guy whose place I had taken was literally seething over what I had inadvertently done. A week later, the foreman settled the matter by assigning me to the task of making microwave oven doors. This was the most difficult spot on the line, where one could barely keep up.

Maybe Galatians 6:9 is the verse for you, "Let us not lose heart in doing good..."

How do you not lose heart when you are penalized for doing good; when you lose clients because you cannot tell a lie; when you are made fun of for your honesty; when you lose a relationship because you will not loosen up?

The rest of Paul's statement to the Galatians prophesies,

Let us not lose heart in doing good, for in due time we will reap if we do not grow weary. (Galatians 6:9)

For the believer who is passionate about holy living, being full of goodness is no small commitment. This is no trite resolution. There is no scamming, no taking advantage of another person, no dishonesty, no shoddy work.

Jesus Christ set the standard; He, "...went about [everywhere] doing good..." (Acts 10:38). We know that when He made a plow or a yoke, He made it to last.

Jesus will one day personally sit at the bema seat. There, for those who mirrored and modeled His character, our Lord will give this commendation,

..."Well done, good and faithful servant..." (Matthew 25:23 KJV)

Becoming a person obsessed with holy living means to radically, entirely, and completely refuse mediocrity.

Radically Refuse Lethargy

...I myself am convinced that you yourselves are full of goodness, filled with all knowledge,... (Romans 15:14)

If a refusal of mediocrity meant you were marked by character; this second phrase means you are marked by conviction.

Now do not misunderstand Paul in this. When he says that the Roman believers are filled with all knowledge, he does not mean that they have nothing else to learn. He means they have all the knowledge they need in order to proceed in their walk with Christ.[2]

In fact, Paul will say in the next verse that they only needed to be reminded of the truths of this letter—indicating they had already received apostolic instruction. More than likely, this came through believers who had been taught by Paul, who now lived in Rome.

Paul is commending these Roman believers for their openness and teachability and passion to learn the things of God.

They were likewise obsessed with the truth of God's Word. Surrounded by paganism, relativism, idolatry, immorality, and corruption on every hand, they had one primary question, "What do the Scriptures say?"

It is no wonder that Paul would open his letter in the first chapter by writing this amazing compliment,

...I thank my God through Jesus Christ for you all, because your faith is being proclaimed throughout the whole world. (Romans 1:8)

Oh to be like the Romans! Has there ever been more of a need for the clarity of the gospel and the conviction of the truth of God than today?

In *World Magazine*, an article covered a story that took place last year. Two researchers from The University of North Carolina at Chapel Hill conducted research in conjunction with the national Study of Youth and Religion. They surveyed 3,000 teenagers about their religious beliefs and published their findings in a new book. They summarized the teens' beliefs with these five statements:

- There is a god who exists who created and ordered the world, but simply watches over human life on earth.
- This god wants people to be nice and fair to each other, as taught by the Bible and most of the world religions.
- This god does not need to be involved in anyone's life, except when he is needed to resolve a problem.
- The central goal of life is to be happy and feel good about yourself.
- Good people go to heaven when they die.

Gene Edward Veith, a Christian columnist, summarized the findings,

Even these secular researchers recognized that this creed is a far cry from true Christianity, with no place for sin, judgment, salvation, or even Jesus Christ. They have a religion of works and a god who does not really care.[3]

In a journal that arrived at my home this week, there was an article on another survey taken by the Harris Organization. It found that 96% of adults who identified themselves as Christians believed that Jesus Christ rose from the dead.

Before you get too excited about this statistic, 50% of the same people believe in the existence of ghosts, 27% of the same people read the horoscope for daily direction, and 21% believe they were someone or something else in a previous life before being reincarnated.[4]

It is no wonder that Paul wrote to the believer,

Be diligent to present yourself approved to God as a workman who does not need to be ashamed, accurately handling the word of truth. (2 Timothy 2:15)

When we put the Bible aside, we throw away our rudder, oars, life jacket, and compass.

Paul wrote to Timothy, "All Scripture is inspired by God [that is, it is the breath of God]; and profitable for teaching [this is what you believe]; for reproof [this tells you where you are wrong]; for correction [this informs you when you are right]; for training in righteousness [this helps you do what is right]; so that the man of God [the believer]; may be adequate, equipped for every good work" (2 Timothy 3:16–17).

Equipped is the Greek word used for a ship that was loaded down with supplies before setting sail. It was also used of a wagon that was packed with all that was necessary before the journey began.

In other words, "Pack the Bible in your wagon, put it on your ship, carry it in your backpack as you head out into life, and you will have all that you need!"

Now I must quickly add that in Romans 15:14, Paul is not necessarily talking about intellectual knowledge or biblical facts. In this text, he uses the word for *knowledge* that means, "to apply what you know or to know by means of application and experience."

Paul wrote,

That I may know Him and the power of His resurrection and the fellowship of His sufferings…(Philippians 3:10)

Wasn't Paul a believer? Didn't he know Christ as his own personal Savior?

Yes! But he used the same word *ginosko*, which implies not mere intellectual activity, but obedient application.

Paul was saying, "I want to know the life of Christ, not just through propositional truth, but through personal testing."

This is the believer who looks into the Word and is among the,

…doers of the Word, and not merely hearers who delude themselves. (James 1:22)

James goes on to say of the one who is an effectual doer,

…not having become a forgetful hearer but an effectual doer, this man will be blessed in what he does. (James 1:25)

I often think of the parable of the CEO who had to leave town on urgent business. He did not have time to meet with his key leadership or any of the employees in his company before leaving, so on his flight out of the country, he wrote a lengthy letter. He informed them that he would be gone for some time, and while he was gone, they were to accomplish a number of things. He ended up being gone for six months.

Without notice, the CEO returned. He pulled into the company parking lot and immediately noticed the weeds growing next to the building. He had left instructions on the landscaping that he wanted done while he was away. As he entered the reception area, he immediately noticed the dust that had collected on the furniture. The receptionist quickly put away her nail file, sat up and said, "Good morning, sir."

He walked past the receptionist, into the warehouse where some of his staff had put up a ping-pong table. The equipment was silent and his staff was involved in what seemed to be a party. They stopped when they saw him and came over to him. He stammered out, "There were things I wanted accomplished, but the equipment is silent, the weeds are growing outside, and the staff is playing instead of working the phones. Didn't you get my letter?"

"Oh, that! You bet, we got it! We made photocopies for every employee and we all took an entire day off just to read it. Man, what a letter! It was great! In fact, we've created smaller groups of employees who meet weekly to discuss the letter. Some of our employees have even memorized parts of the letter. It is so good!"

Then, everyone fell quiet under the gaze of the CEO. He asked, "Did you do what I told you to do in the letter?"

"Oh, no sir. You see, sir, we're still studying the letter."

Paul is commending the Roman believers for refusing this kind of dichotomy; this kind of contradiction.

He commends them for refusing lethargy; for refusing the urge to examine the truth, but never execute the truth; to analyze the Bible, but not apply the Bible; to read the Word, without every reproducing the Word in life.

Go deeply in your study of the Word—just make sure you surface. What good does it do if your depth in the Word does not become a demonstration of the truth of God's Word.

Radically Refuse Apathy

...I myself am convinced that you yourselves are full of goodness, filled with all knowledge, and able also to admonish one another. (Romans 15:14)

The word "admonish" is from *noutheteo*, which gives us our word "nouthetic." Jay Adams popularized the concept of "nouthetic counseling" in his book entitled, *Competent to Counsel*. The meaning, taken directly from this title is "able to counsel."

The word *noutheteo* is a compound Greek word made up of *nous*, meaning, "mind or intellect," and *tithemi*, meaning, "to put or place." When these are put together, it gives the idea of conveying something into someone's mind or someone's understanding which will correct them. This is like our common expression, "Let me lay something on your mind."

The words "teaching and admonishing" appear together in Paul's writings. He tells us that the believers are to be,

...teaching and admonishing one another... (Colossians 3:16)

The word "teach" seems to be used most often as a positive declaration, while "admonish" seems to be used with a more corrective meaning.

"Admonish one another," Paul wrote to the Romans. Literally, this meant, "correct one another." It has the idea of stirring one another up.

Why? Because we have the tendency to settle down into a rut. We are creatures of habit—we go home the same way; we eat the same things; we have our routine. We even sit in the same seats in class or in church.[5]

I can remember in elementary school thinking that my name was "Settle Down." Every time Mrs. Jolly or Mrs. Stickle saw me, they would invariably have to say, "Hey you, settle down....You, settle down." I figured that was my middle name, Stephen Settle-Down Davey!

The trouble is—when you get old enough, you start listening to that advice. You not only settle down, you wear down.

Yet the Christian life is called a race; a war; a match. It calls for discipline, drive, and determination.

We need one another to provoke each other. We need prodding, stirring up, and admonishing because we tend to float in the current. Even worse, we tend to slide away.

D. A. Carson wrote,

We do not drift toward holiness. We do not gravitate toward godliness, prayer, obedience to Scripture, faith, and delight in the Lord. We drift toward compromise and call it tolerance; we drift toward disobedience and call it freedom; we drift toward superstition and call it faith. We cherish the lack of discipline and call it relaxation; we slouch toward prayerlessness and think we have escaped legalism; we slide toward godlessness and convince ourselves we have been liberated.[6]

It is no wonder we need to admonish one another—to provoke each other and challenge one another to live for Christ.

I received a letter this week, from a young lady in another part of the state who listens to *Wisdom for the Heart*. She thanked us for the book she had received, which she finished in just a few days. Every time the program comes on the air, she gets out her Bible and her notebook and takes as many notes as she can. She asked several questions in her letter, which was addressed to me. She asked questions about how to discover the will of God for her life. You can easily tell, by her letter, that she is passionate about living for Christ. She writes, "I'll do anything God tells me to do. I often tell the Lord, 'Lord, show me what to do. I am totally open to you.' "

What challenged me the most about this letter is that it was written by a young lady who happens to be in middle school! She is not even a teenager yet!

She signed the letter, "Your friend in the Lord."

Paul would say of this young lady, as he said of the Roman believers, and I trust, would say of you and me, "We are people who make three radical refusals in our quest for holy living for the glory of God. We will refuse mediocrity—we will not settle for second class workmanship. We will refuse lethargy—we will not stop with learning the Word without living the Word. We will refuse apathy—we will care enough to cheer one another on in this race we call the Christian life."

We will make these refusals whether it is through a phone conversation, a Bible lesson, an arm around the shoulder, or perhaps a card or a letter like the one from this young lady that ends with the words, "Your friend in the Lord."

It is true, what Robert Murray McCheyne once wrote,

It is not great talent that God blesses so much as great likeness to Jesus Christ. A holy [Christian] is an awesome weapon in the hand of God.

[1] J. Harrison Hudson, *"The Impact of Robert Murray McCheyne," Life and Work,* (Jan., 1987).

[2] R. C. H. Lenski, *The Interpretation of St. Paul's Epistle to the Romans* (Augsburg, 1945), p. 877.

[3] Gene Edward Veith, "A Nation of Deists," *World Magazine* (June 25, 2005).

[4] "Casper Friendly Theology," *Leadership Magazine* (Spring 2006).

[5] John Phillips, *Exploring Romans* (Moody Press, 1969), p. 253.

[6] D. A. Carson, "Reflections," *Christianity Today* (July 31, 2000).

Gripped by Grace
Romans 15:15–16

Tucked inside his personal resumé, we discover Paul's obsession with the grace of God.

> *But I have written very boldly to you on some points, so as to remind you again, because of the grace that was given me from God, to be a minister of Christ Jesus to the Gentiles, ministering as a priest the gospel of God, so that my offering of the Gentiles may become acceptable, sanctified by the Holy Spirit. (Romans 15:15–16)*

In this brief resumé, Paul either implies or directly refers to three different roles that he played in life. These roles are that of professor, preacher, and priest. All of these roles are the direct result of grace.

If you bumped into Paul, he would spill grace. If you talked to Paul, he would speak grace. If you prayed with Paul, he would appeal to the grace of God.

I agree with one author who said that Paul never fully recovered from his conversion. Paul was gripped by the saving grace of God.

Max Lucado published a devotional book several years ago, with this title, *In the Grip of Grace*. He began the book by telling a story he had created to declare the truths of grace; a story he entitled, "The Parable of the River."

Once there were five sons who lived in a mountain castle with their father. The eldest was an obedient son, but his four younger brothers were rebellious. Their father had warned them of the river, but the younger sons had not listened.

The father had begged these four rebellious sons to stay clear of the bank, lest they be swept downstream, but the river's lure was too strong. Each day they ventured closer and closer, until one son dared to reach in and feel the waters. "Hold my hand so I won't fall in," he said, and his brothers did.

However, when he touched the water, the current yanked all four of the brothers into the rapids and rolled them down the river. Over rocks they bounced, through the channels they roared, on the swells they rode. Their cries for help were lost in the rage of the river. After hours of struggle, they surrendered to the pull of the river and finally found themselves dumped on the bank of a strange land, in a distant country, in a barren place.

After some time, they gathered their courage and reentered the waters. The brothers were hoping to walk upstream, but the current was too strong. They attempted to walk along the river's edge, but the terrain was too steep. They considered climbing the mountains, but the peaks were too high. Besides, they did not know the way.

Lucado goes on to talk about one of the brothers moving in with the barbarians in the valley below, building his own hut of mud and grass. He decided that life with the pagans was better than life with his father.

Another brother became bitter and decided to simply watch his other brother and report all the bad things he did.

A third brother decided that the only way back to his father was to build a path back up the river and walk back. He said, "There is only this option. Rock upon rock I will stack until I have enough rocks to travel upstream to the castle of my father. When he sees how hard I have worked and how diligent I have been, he will have no choice but to open the door and let me into his house."

After several days, a rescuer appears. It is the firstborn son. But tragically, every one of his brothers rejects his offer of help.

The brother living with the barbarians has grown to prefer his life with them.

The brother who has grown bitter and only wants to watch the failure and the sin of the barbarians and of his brother is also too preoccupied to be rescued.

The brother who is building a path upstream has been able to take five steps homeward, of which he is very proud, but when the rescuer tells him there are five million steps to go, he grows angry and begins to throw rocks at his oldest brother. In spite of the possibility of rescue, he prefers to work his way home and earn his father's forgiveness, and thus, rejects the firstborn son.[1]

Look back at Paul's history as a faithful Hebrew, a fearless patriot of the Law, and a meticulous keeper of all the regulations and ceremonies of his Jewish people. He would have been the brother on the river bank, working unceasingly at the futile task of building a path to heaven out of the rocks of man-made righteousness. He had walked five steps, but had five million to go.

Paul experienced saving grace on that pathway, while heading to Damascus to arrest the Christians who dared to suggest that the crucified carpenter was the Son of God. In a flash of light from the sky, the appearance of Christ to Paul brought divine illumination. While he physically went blind for several days, he gained spiritual sight. He was brought to life through faith in his newly found Lord, Jesus Christ.

Paul would later write his testimony,

Circumcised the eighth day, of the nation of Israel, of the tribe of Benjamin, a Hebrew of Hebrews; as to the Law, a Pharisee; as to zeal, a persecutor of the church; as to the righteousness which is in the Law, found blameless. But whatever things were gain to me, those things I have counted as loss for the sake of Christ. (Philippians 3:5-7)

After his conversion, Paul began a remarkable ministry that has continued to impact the church for nearly two thousand years.

What were the roles Paul played as he demonstrated his rescue by grace? Paul writes that by God,

...I was appointed a preacher and an apostle and a teacher. (2 Timothy 1:11)

It was Paul's job to be a teacher or professor. It was Paul's jurisdiction to be a preacher to the Gentiles. It was Paul's joy to be a priest unto God.

Paul, the Professor

But I have written very boldly to you on some points so as to remind you again... (Romans 15:15)

A teacher's most powerful tool before the exam may very well be the review sheet. When the final exams are just around the corner, the students are all ears.

I do not know about you, but I had the terrible habit of ignoring the lectures in class and simply waiting for the review. Of course, I never made the dean's list either.

I have had military personnel tell me that a soldier listens to a review of his equipment much differently at his assigned destination than he did while at the base.

I have counseled dozens of couples who plan to get married, and the way they listen to me in my office is vastly different than the way they listen to me in the ceremony when I deliver the charge.

I could preach this Sunday on death and dying; heaven and hell, but the audience would not listen as well as an audience at a funeral. Ask any pastor and they will tell you that an audience's attention at a funeral service is unrivaled.

There is something about being reminded when you really need to know.

- That student wants to pass the exam!
- That soldier is about to go into battle!
- That couple is about to become husband and wife!
- That audience is face to face with a coffin and they want to know about eternal life!

The Roman believers were surrounded by the challenges and difficulties of building not only their lives, but also a church. They needed to know! So like a great professor, Paul gave them a number of review sheets to help us pass the exams of life.

With these and other believers, Paul often spent time reminding them of the truths of grace.

Paul had spent three years teaching the Ephesian believers, establishing the elders as shepherds, and then, in his farewell, he exhorts them to

> *...remember the words of the Lord Jesus, that He Himself said, "It is more blessed to give than to receive." (Acts 20:35b)*

Paul challenged the Galatians to join him in being eager to

> *...remember the poor... (Galatians 2:10).*

As Timothy struggled in his ministry as a young and inexperienced pastor, Paul encouraged him to

> *...remember Jesus Christ, risen from the dead...for which I [Paul] suffer hardship even to imprisonment... (2 Timothy 2:8–9).*

In addition, in this same letter Paul reminded Timothy of the gifts of power, love, and discipline that God had given him to use in the ministry (2 Timothy 1:7); the fact that God has saved them and called them according to His own purpose and grace (2 Timothy 1:9); the truth that to those who believe, the Savior has abolished death and brought life and immortality to light through the gospel (2 Timothy 1:10); the remembrance that he was not ashamed of the gospel; for he knew whom he had believed and was convinced that He is able to guard what He had entrusted to Paul until that day (1 Timothy 1:12); the reminder, concerning the preaching of this gospel to retain the standard of sound words (1 Timothy 1:15).

One of the best things you can do to refresh your holy obsession for God is remember.

This is like the prophet Isaiah, who said,

Listen to me, you who...seek [to follow] the Lord: look to the rock from which you were hewn and to the excavation of [the] pit from which you were dug. (Isaiah 51:1)

This is like David the Psalmist who sang,

He brought me up out of the pit of destruction, out of the miry clay, and He set my feet upon a rock...(Psalm 40:2)

Why do you think the Lord delivered to the church only one ordinance to repeat over and over? It is the one we do as often as we choose when we assemble, and we call it the Lord's Table of Remembrance. We do this ordinance to *remember* Him!

Now notice that Paul the professor is speaking boldly to the Romans.

But I have written very boldly to you on some points... (Romans 15:15a)

Why was there the need for boldness?

For one thing, a person who already knows what you are telling them could grow frustrated or even upset that you are reminding them of what they already know.

This is like the teenager who does not like to be reminded again and again, "Drive safely," or "Be careful." Their parents get the answer, "I know, Dad," or "I know, Mom."

It is one thing to tell a child, "2 + 2 = 4" when he did not already know it. It is another thing to tell that to Einstein.

It is one thing to tell a fourth grade computer class, "Now, class, here's what a right click on a mouse will do." It is entirely different to tell Bill Gates, "Here's what a mouse can do."

A teacher runs the risk of boring the students and being ignored.

This past week, I had the delight of welcoming into my office all of the three and four year old preschool classes at our church. One of the teachers had asked me if I would come and meet the children and their teachers and perhaps, speak at their chapel service.

I said, "Sure, I'd love to, but how about another idea? Why don't we have them come to my office and let me talk to them and show them my office and my books? I have about a thousand books on either side of my desk that I could show them. Maybe I could tell them what a pastor does and even show them some of the treasures I've collected from mission fields of the world."

So, this past week, four classes of three and four year olds visited me in my office. They came through, one at a time, for about ten minutes each. The teachers stood at the back and the kids gathered around my desk and my chair.

Every class had a talker; a natural leader who asked all the questions and volunteered information—information I did not want to know. I learned about many of the marriages in our church. I had my secretary set up numerous counseling sessions later that week!

Anyway, after showing them my carved ostrich egg from India, one little girl, who just seemed so enamored by the whole thing, raised her hand. "Oh, oh," she said.

I said, "Yes ma'am, and what do you want to ask me?"

She said, "Um, can we get outta here now?!"

I was a huge success!

A professor runs the risk of boring his students with stuff they already know or stuff they do not care to know anything about.

Obviously the Roman believers welcomed the review and, like us today, would love to have been given even more on their review sheet.

Paul, the Preacher

...because of the grace that was given me from God, to be a minister of Christ Jesus to the Gentiles...(Romans 15:15b–16a)

Paul's job may have been to be a teacher, but his jurisdiction was to be a preacher to the Gentiles.

Paul was given a special responsibility for the Gentiles. In Galatians 2:1–10, we are told that Peter primarily preached to the Jews and Paul primarily preached to the Gentiles. The predominant influencer of the church—this brand-new organism; the body of Christ—was not Peter, but Paul.

Soon after Paul was converted on the road to Damascus, the Lord said to Ananias in a vision that,

…he [Paul] is a chosen instrument of Mine, to bear My name before the Gentiles…(Acts 9:15)

In the first chapter of Romans, Paul revealed that God had made him an apostle,

…to bring about the obedience of faith among all the Gentiles…(Romans 1:5)

We could correctly say that the Gentiles were the primary jurisdiction of Paul's preaching influence.

Notice that Paul does not say that he has been appointed as the chief instrument of Christ because of his superior intellect, or his speaking ability, or his background in the law, or his personality, or anything like that.[2]

Paul directly links his preaching office to the fact that he is the recipient of the grace of God. He is gripped with the truth that God's grace has not only redeemed him, but has ordained him.

Perhaps this is the reason that Paul does not flash his credentials as an apostle to the Roman church. He does not say, "Hey, listen, I'm not only your professor, I'm an apostle."

Notice that Paul does not say, "I am an apostle of Christ Jesus to the Gentiles." Instead, he says,

…[I am] a minister of Christ Jesus to the Gentiles… *(Romans 15:16)*

The word he uses comes out of sheer humility. The word "minister" is the Greek word *leitourgos,* which gives us our English word, "liturgy."

The word originally referred to someone who served a public office at his own expense.[3]

In other words, there is no salary, no pension, no benefit package with this office—just service for the public good out of a generous heart.

Over time, this word came to refer to someone who volunteered to serve their country or their city in some way. I found several ancient examples of what it meant to be a *leitourgos*.

Greek cities had great festivals each year that included music and drama. Men who loved their city would volunteer to collect, instruct, and equip a chorus at their own expense.

The Athenians were the greatest naval power of the ancient world. One of the most patriotic things that a wealthy man could do was underwrite the expenses of one warship for a whole year. This was an incredible sacrifice for the good of his country.

The word was also used in relation to the Athenian games. During these festival games, there would be the famous torch races. The Athenians would be divided into ten tribes. In these races, teams from the tribes would race each other in relay races and the runners would actually carry a lit torch. To this day, we speak of handing off the torch to the next in line. These games were paid for by *leitourgos*—men who not only paid the expenses, but spent time selecting and training the athletes to represent their tribe.

Over time the word was associated with people who performed religious duties. More than likely this was because the duties were voluntary.

Out of this came the translation "minister," which was a reference to someone who handled the liturgies of the church.[4]

Paul is announcing that he views himself as so gripped by grace that he is willing to pour out all that he owns and all that he is for the sake of his new family; his new tribe; his new country. No matter what the cost, no matter how much time it demanded, he was willing to sacrifice everything to win the race; to pass on the torch; to equip the ship and fight the good fight of faith; to train the church to sing praise to God. It did not matter to him if it cost him his life.

Like most physicians of great experience, Dr. Evan Kane had become preoccupied with a particular facet of medicine. His strong feelings concerned the use of general anesthesia in major surgery.

Dr. Kane believed that most major operations could and should be performed under a local anesthetic, for in his opinion, the hazards of general anesthesia outweighed the risks of the surgery itself. His medical mission was to prove to his colleagues, once and for all, that local anesthesia was worth exploring.

To prove the viability of major surgery using only a local anesthetic, Kane would have to find a patient brave enough to go through a major surgery without general anesthesia. In his thirty-seven years as a surgeon, Kane had performed nearly four thousand appendectomies. It was not long before he found a patient who needed an appendectomy, and would volunteer to take the risk of only local anesthesia.

The patient was prepped in all the normal ways, but in the operating room was given only a local anesthetic. As he had thousands of times before, Dr. Kane entered the abdomen, slicing tissue and clamping blood vessels as he operated on his patient. Locating the appendix, the surgeon skillfully clipped it away, folded the stump back in place, and sewed up the patient's wound—all with the patient being fully awake and experiencing only minor discomfort. After two days of recovery—much faster than general anesthesia cases—the patient was released from the hospital to recuperate at home.

Dr. Kane had achieved his goal. His patient was too credible a testimony to deny or ignore. You see, Dr. Evan Kane had operated on himself. He was the only patient he could find willing to take the risk and make the sacrifice.

Since this surgery in 1921, Dr. Kane's breakthrough technique changed the face of surgery and saved the lives of countless numbers of people.[5]

Is it any wonder that the people of God who make the most difference in our lives are not the ones who walk around flashing their credentials to remind us of how much they know and how much they matter? Instead, they are typically volunteers who offer their bodies, their hearts, their bank accounts, and their time to save countless lives.

Like Paul, the people of God who make the most difference are enamored by the grace of God and the God of grace.

Paul, the Priest

As a professor, Paul was clearly motivated by grace; as a preacher, Paul delivered the message of grace; as a priest, Paul was involved in the miracle of grace.

...to be a minister of Christ Jesus to the Gentiles, ministering as a priest the gospel of God, so that my offering of the Gentiles may become acceptable, sanctified by the Holy Spirit. (Romans 15:16)

If being a professor was Paul's job, and preaching to the Gentiles was Paul's jurisdiction, then, being a priest unto God was Paul's joy.

As a priest in this dispensation of grace, Paul was not offering up a lamb or a grain offering. The text tells us that he was offering up to God Gentile converts; he was offering to God this miracle of grace—sanctified Gentile believers.[6]

What mattered most to Paul were the people. It was not his job, not his jurisdiction, not even his own sense of satisfaction and joy that mattered the most to Paul, but sanctified, growing, separated, holy, maturing disciples.

What a great challenge to everyone who is also a priest unto God—for Christ,

...has made us to be...priests to His God and Father... (Revelation 1:6)

This also is our joy.

We can easily become preoccupied with the programs we administer, the subject matter we teach, the books we read or write, and forget that the purpose of all the programs, classes, books, lessons, and activities is nothing less than the formation of strong Christians—sanctified Christians; that is, set apart and holy, acceptable offerings unto God, which is our reasonable service.[7]

Paul saw himself dressed in priestly garments, even though he was involved in the dusty, mundane business of traveling the ancient world on foot, while suffering from exposure, threats, beatings, and rejection. He saw himself dressed in priestly garb, in the holy of holies, lifting up the souls of men, ascending as sweet smelling savor to almighty God.

This view made the most mundane daily occurrences holy. It meant, all of life was liturgy.

Paul was gripped by the grace of God, serving with grace the people of God for the glory of God.

If only we could see our service like this then our lives would be filled the same holy obsession. A pie baked for a neighbor becomes an offering to God; a child loved is an act of worship; an employee treated with dignity becomes a hymn of praise; the gospel shared with an unbeliever becomes a sweet gift to God; a Sunday school class becomes a holy place where you handle sacred things.

This is the sacred view of life…this is what it means to become gripped by grace; this is holy obsession.[8]

It led one believer to make this commitment to Christ, "The will of God: nothing less; nothing more; nothing else."

Another believer who lived for Christ, said it this way, "No reserve! No regrets! No retreat!"

They have become gripped by the love and grace of the Lord, and this grace is so amazing it demands my soul, my life, my all.

This is living with holy obsession. This is saying,

> *The will of God,*
> *The work of God,*
> *The name of God,*
> *The leadership of God,*
> *The honor and glory of God,*
> *nothing less; nothing more; nothing else.*

I believe this is what it means to be gripped by the grace of God.

---

[1] Max Lucado, *In the Grip of Grace* (Word Publishers, 1996), p. 1.

[2] R. C. H. Lenski, *The Interpretation of St. Paul's Epistle to the Romans* (Augsburg Publishing, 1945), p. 878.

[3] Ralph Earle, *Word Meanings in the New Testament* (Baker, 1974), p. 205.

[4] William Barclay, *The Letter to the Romans* (Westminster Press, 1975), p. 202.

[5] Kenneth Boa and William Kruidenier, Holman *New Testament Commentary: Romans* (Holman, 2000), p. 445.

[6] R. Kent Hughes, *Romans: Righteousness from Heaven* (Crossway Books), 1991, p. 288.

[7] Clinton Arnold, *Zondervan Illustrated Bible Backgrounds Commentary* (Zondervan, 2002), p. 88.

[8] Hughes, p. 288.

The Magnification of the Master
Romans 15:17–19

When Chan Gailey was the head coach of Alabama's Troy State football team, they were the unlikely team playing for a National Championship. In the week before the big game, interview requests were pouring in from everywhere.

A few days before the championship, Gailey was heading to the practice field when his secretary wanted to transfer a call to him. Somewhat irritated, he told her to take a message because he was on his way to practice. She responded "Are you sure? It's *Sports Illustrated.*"

"I'll be right there," he said.

As Gailey made his way back to his office, he began to think about the article. It would be great publicity for the program at Troy State—in fact, three pages would not be enough to cover the great story.

Getting closer to his office, Gailey started thinking that he might even end up on the cover. "Wow…should I pose or go with some kind of action shot," he wondered. His head was spinning with all the possibilities.

When he picked up the phone and said, "Hello," the person asked, "Is this Chan Gailey?"

"Yes, it is," he replied with a measure of pride.

"This is *Sports Illustrated*, and we're calling to let you know your subscription is running out...do you want to renew?"

Coach Gailey concluded the story by saying, "You are either humble or you will be humbled by life."[1]

This is a good truth to remember for there is nothing more harmful to a believer than too much of himself. Preening in front of a rear view mirror usually causes accidents.

There is nothing more damaging to relationships and the work of Christ than the spirit of Diotrephes, who, as John the Apostle wrote,

...loves to be first [preeminent]...(3 John 1:9).

John the Baptizer, on the other hand, got it right when he said of Christ,

He must increase, but I must decrease. (John 3:30)

The antidote to the poison of self is the glory of Christ.

The tragedy of the church at-large in the past twenty-five years is that it openly and unashamedly made the human being the object of attention. We are now constantly looking into the mirror—not of the Word, but of our world. In the average church today, Christ is decreasing and we are increasing.

The more we stare at ourselves; the more we twist the motive for assembling into self-help sessions; the more we turn the Bible into quick and easy principles for successful, comfortable living; the more self-centered we become, and since we can never be satisfied with ourselves, our dissatisfaction only grows greater.

The way to improve life is not a better understanding of who we are, but a better understanding of who God is. The cure for what ails us is not necessarily thinking less about ourselves, but thinking more about Him.

We do not need a better view of ourselves, we need a fresh vision; a newly kindled obsession with the glory of God. We then would say, as Moses did,

> ...*[Lord], show me Your glory! (Exodus 33:18)*

In a little book I keep on my desk at home, entitled, *The Supremacy of God in Preaching*, John Piper writes,

> People are starving for the grandeur of God. And even those who go to church—how many of them can say when they leave, "I have looked upon You, oh God, in the sanctuary, beholding Your...glory." (Psalm 63:2)[2]

What is the glory of God? It is the sum and substance of His character; the beauty of His holiness; and the revelation of God in Christ—for when He came to dwell among us,

> ...*we saw His glory, glory as of the only begotten from the Father, full of grace and truth. (John 1:14)*

Paul reminded the Corinthians that the glory of God was the main point of apostolic preaching, when he wrote,

> ...*we do not preach ourselves but Christ Jesus as Lord...* *(2 Corinthians 4:5)*

In the next verse, Paul said that the glory of God was the subject of our ongoing study,

...God...is the One who has shone in our hearts to give the light of the knowledge of the glory of God...(2 Corinthians 4:6)

Imagine, on the evening when the shepherds were tending their flocks, when an angel appeared before them and,

...the glory of the Lord shone around them...(Luke 2:9)

You might say, "I wish I could see what that's like!"

You will! That element of God's glory will one day be tangibly revealed to us all in the heavenly city. John the apostle wrote,

...the city has no need of the sun or of the moon to shine on it, for the glory of God has illumined it... (Revelation 21:23)

Even today,

The heavens are telling of the glory of God...(Psalm 19:1)

Honoring and exaltating God is the objective of everything we do, for in

...whatever you do, do all to the glory of God. (1 Corinthians 10:31)

In other words, we are to do everything to the exaltation of God; the honor of God; the pleasure of God; the leading and sovereign right of God.

In a very plain sense, living for the glory of God means that in everything, we emphasize Him and de-emphasize ourselves.

This is like Raymond Lull, a missionary to the Muslims many years ago. He lived by the life-long refrain, "I have one passion—it is He, it is He, it is He."[3]

The glory of God is our goal, our subject, our hope, our delight, our message, and our future. This is what it means to be obsessed with the glory of God.

Delighted in Elevating the Person of Christ

Therefore in Christ Jesus I have found reason for boasting in things pertaining to God. (Romans 15:17)

Paul delighted in elevating the person and work of Jesus Christ; he refused to make himself the primary topic of conversation. We cannot be obsessed with God's glory and our own glory at the same time. These are mutually exclusive preoccupations. We cannot promote His reputation and our reputation at the same time.

This verse is Paul's way of saying, "Allow me to brag about Jesus Christ. Let me boast of Christ." This is difficult to do if we are wanting to add to the prayer list our latest spiritual achievement.

More often, we are like the Little Leaguer who put all his sixty pounds into a ferocious swing and barely connected. The ball scraped by the bottom of the bat, jiggled straight back to the pitcher, who fumbled it and then, threw it over the first baseman's head. The slugger flew on toward second base. Somebody retrieved the ball, but threw it over the second baseman's head into left field. The hitter rounded third as another throw went to second base, and he touched home plate as the ball sailed past the catcher. He was heard to say, "That's the first home run I ever hit in my whole life."

That little boy is us; we step to the plate for Jesus, barely tip the ball, He arranges everything so we make it around the bases and then, we announce at the prayer meeting how we managed to pull it off![4]

Paul would write,

…may it never be that I would boast, except in the cross of our Lord Jesus Christ…(Galatians 6:14)

This is the magnification of the Master.

Declined the Pedestal of Human Praise

For I will not presume to speak of anything except what Christ has accomplished through me, resulting in the obedience of the Gentiles by word and deed. (Romans 15:18)

This is just like Paul—he refuses to accept personal credit for spiritual fruit.

Gentile masses are coming to faith in Christ and obeying the truth of the gospel and Paul is the signature spokesman. However, he writes, in effect, "Don't put me on a pedestal; don't elevate me, elevate Christ working in me. I wouldn't even presume to talk about anything I've done, without putting it in the context of Christ working through me."

Open the New Testament and read, you will soon discover that Paul had more reason to boast than any of the other apostles, including Peter and John. He was used by God to reveal more of the New Testament than any other human writer, and the greater part of the book of Acts focuses on his ministry.[5]

If anybody deserved to be on the cover of a magazine—*Time Magazine's* Missionary of the Century—it would be Paul.

There is no doubt among Bible-believing Christians that Paul was, and still is, the most influential Christian author, theologian, pastor, and teacher of all time. He impacted the world.

I found it interesting that the Christian Science Monitor reported last year that there are more than 100 books in print with titles that include the phrase "that changed the world." Some of the titles include:

- Gunpowder: The History of the Explosive that Changed the World.
- El Nino: The Weather Phenomenon that Changed the World.
- The Pill: A Biography of the Drug that Changed the World.
- Mauve: How One Man Invented a Color that Changed the World.
- The Twist: The Song and Dance that Changed the World.
- Cod: A Biography of the Fish that Changed the World.
- Model T Ford: The Car that Changed the World.

We live in the land of the overstated and the easily impressed, but this is the way the world works. Make any impression; create any trend; make any discovery; start any fad;

lead an organization; make strides in any field and the pedestal awaits—expect it, welcome it, make the most of it. The more visible you are, the less real you can become.

By now, it should be Paul the celebrity. He can do anything.

The press reports of one communist country's leader would be almost laughable—if they were not so tragic. North Korea's leader is presented as brilliant, perfect, and gifted. MSNBC reported last year that the press in his Stalinist state promote him as the greatest man—perfect in every way. He supposedly goes through daily intensive memory sessions and can now, as he himself said, "remember all the computer codes and telephone numbers of government workers." In spite of his busy schedule, he evidently has the time to compose entire operas and produce movies. North Korean propaganda stretched too far recently, however, when it reported that their leader played golf for the very first time in his life and in that round of golf, shot eleven holes-in-one.[6]

This is the mentality of human nature—he is the great leader, so he must be great at everything!

Listen to the great leader of the church, as he refuses this kind of press report. He demonstrates an unwillingness to step up on the pedestal that everyone would assume he had the right to mount.

...I will not presume to speak of anything except what Christ has accomplished through me... (Romans 15:18)

He writes to the Corinthian believers,

...I will rather boast about my weaknesses, so that the power of Christ may dwell in me. Therefore I am well content with weaknesses, with insults, with distresses, with persecutions, with difficulties, for Christ's sake; for when I am weak, then I am strong. (2 Corinthians 12:9b–10)

Follow the progression of Paul's own growth as God became greater and greater to him over time, and Paul became more and more the object of God's grace.

Paul referred to himself as, "...the least of the apostles..." (1 Corinthians 15:9). Later Paul wrote that he considered himself, "...the very least of all saints..." (Ephesians 3:8). Finally, near the end of his life, Paul wrote, "...sinners, among whom I am foremost of all" (1 Timothy 1:15).

Donald Grey Barnhouse summarized what Paul could have easily gloried in:

Paul had this ability to enter a completely pagan city which practiced devil worship and gather a group of transformed believers in the name of Christ. He then hovered over them in prayer and, by constant admonition, lifted them from the most corrupt stratum of heathenism to the highest level of Christian godliness and morality.[7]

Certainly Paul does not deny what God has done with him and through him, nor does Paul belittle it either—that would be false humility. But at the end of the day, he teaches that we are all simply instruments in the hand of God, and no Christian should ever look for the pedestal for what God does through him. The pedestal belongs to God alone.

No paint brush can take credit for the masterpiece it was used to paint. No violin takes credit for the beautiful music the musician makes with it.[8]

As a young man, one Christian composer and singer who was popular in England had become proud of his accomplishments and his fame. He and other singers and musicians formed a small group that led music for his home church. On one occasion, their pastor confronted them with what he perceived to be pride in their musical ability and performance. He told them that they had lost the reason they were doing what they were doing and had neglected true worship.

These musicians were insulted by the charge and every one of them packed their instruments and left the church—all, that is, except this one young man. Soon afterward, he wrote the song that for several years, has been sung on two continents. It is a prayer of confession and rededication to the Lord that acknowledges that the Lord wants more than a song—He wants a life. Some of the lyrics in this prayer to the Lord are, "I'm coming back to the heart of worship and Lord, it's all about You."[9]

This is Paul's perspective. He is intent on magnifying his Master—Jesus Christ.

Directed the Spotlight on the Holy Spirit

In the power of signs and wonders, in the power of the Spirit; so that from Jerusalem and round about as far as Illyricum I have fully preached the gospel of Christ. (Romans 15:9)

Paul informs us of the truth that the apostolic community had the authenticating miracle-working power to demonstrate that they were indeed servants of the living God.

A *sign* simply served to mark something. The shepherds were told, as a sign, the baby would be wrapped in swaddling clothes and lying in a manger (Luke 2:12). *Wonders* were just that—they caused people to marvel. Combining wonders with signs gave spiritual significance to the marvel of the miracle. Signs and wonders were badges of apostolic authenticity.

Paul clearly stated that they were for the apostles to use, when he wrote,

The signs of a true apostle were performed among you with all perseverance, by signs and wonders and miracles. (2 Corinthians 12:12)

In Paul's day, the New Testament had yet to be completed. Paul never heard the Sermon on the Mount or read John 3:16. He could never pick up a copy of 1 Peter or Jude or James. He had never heard of the book of Revelation, because it had not been written yet.[10]

The badge of authenticity was Paul's ability to heal the sick and give sight to the blind and raise the dead.

Without signs and wonders, before the Scriptures were completed, the apostles would have lacked any verifying evidence that they were truly of God, as they laid the foundation of the church in this dispensation of grace. So God in His providence, gave to His apostles the same ability Christ had demonstrated—they did the same things He did—they gave sight to the blind, raised the crippled to walk again, and raised the dead. It was an undeniable sign of God's favor and seal.

Today, we are not laying the foundation of the apostles—we are building on their foundation. The verifying seal and sign of God's approval on any preacher or teacher today is their association with the Word of God. Now the litmus test is true doctrine.

The test of whether or not a man is a herald for God depends upon his connection *to* and explanation *of* Scripture. Why? Because the Word of God is now sufficient to prepare every Christian for every good work (2 Timothy 3:16–17).

Someone once said to Barnhouse that it was not fair that we could not turn water into wine anymore or do other miracles of that nature. Barnhouse said, "I've seen an even greater miracle than that—I've seen an alcoholic father of a newborn little girl give his heart to Jesus Christ, and by the power of the gospel, we saw whiskey turned into milk."[11]

However, go back in time to when the apostle Paul lived and served. Imagine being at a testimony meeting with the assembly when Paul is in the audience.

"Anybody have a testimony of something God has done for you or through you?"

"Yes, Paul?"

"It was so amazing in Lystra, where that man who had been crippled from birth was listening to me preach. I looked at him and then, with all the courage I could muster—right out there where everyone could hear and know whether or not I had the power of God—I said to him, 'Stand up and walk.' He leapt to his feet and the people began calling me Jupiter—one of their gods. Man, that was so exciting!"

"Anybody else have a testimony? Yes, Paul—another?"

"Oh, let me tell you about that demon-possessed girl in Philippi. She kept following me around, and it was so annoying. Finally, I turned to her and simply commanded the demon, 'In the name of Jesus Christ, come out!' and the demon came out. Wow, what power!"

"Hey, do you want to hear the one about the guy I raised from the dead?"

Who could follow that?

However, in case you missed it, Paul inserted the phrase, "…in the power of the Spirit…" (Romans 15:19).

This could be read, "in connection with the Holy Spirit's power."

In other words, Paul is saying, "It wasn't me—it was the Spirit of God at work in me and through me."

Paul was obsessed with the glory of God and did not want in any way to rob God of praise or glory. He delighted to elevate the person of Christ, he declined to be placed on a pedestal of human praise, and he directed the spotlight of attention on the person of the Holy Spirit. More than anything, Paul wanted the magnification of his Master to be obvious to everyone.

I was reminded of a story I read some time ago, about a well-known Christian leader who was picked up by a seminary student at the airport. The student was awed to be in the car with this man and he offered compliments and then plied him with questions. This leader refused to accept any accolade—almost distancing himself from his successful ministry. Finally, the young man said, "Surely you see yourself and your gifts as the primary factors in your ministry's success."

The older gentleman paused and then, said, "Young man, when I was growing up on the farm, I had to walk to school and back every weekday. I'd walk along a pasture where there was a wooden fence with long wooden rails attached to fence posts every ten feet or so. One day, I remember coming across a turtle perched up on top of one of those fence posts. I knew someone had put him there; a turtle can't climb a fence and get there by himself, you know. Son, I am nothing more than a turtle on a fencepost."

This is what is called refusing the pedestal of praise, redirecting the spotlight, magnifying the Master as a result of being captivated by and dedicated to the glory of God.

This is good news for every ordinary Christian—and the truth is, we are all very ordinary. Whether you are well-known or unknown, God's truth is displayed through the simple; God's strength is revealed to the weak; and God's grace is distributed to the needy.

God's glory is magnified when weak, simple, needy, ordinary Christians praise Him and refuse the pedestal; love Him and redirect the praise to Him; worship Him and elevate His name above any other name.

We are ordinary Christians who are nothing more than turtles placed on fence posts—and when asked, we will magnify our Master, for we are obsessed with the glory of God.

[1] Chan Gailey, http://www.preachingtoday.com, 4/20/2004.

[2] John Piper, *The Supremacy of God in Preaching* (Baker Books, 1990), p. 107.

[3] R. Kent Hughes, *Romans* (Crossway Books, 1991), p. 290.

[4] Ibid., p. 289.

[5] John MacArthur, *Romans* (Moody Press, 1994), p. 333.

[6] http://www.msnbc.msn.com, 8/2/05.

[7] James Boice, *Romans: Volume 4* (Baker Books, 1995), p. 1863.

[8] MacArthur, p. 335.

[9] "Midday Connection," *Moody Broadcasting Network*, 11/28/2001.

[10] Donald Grey Barnhouse, *Romans: Volume 4* (Eerdmans, 1964), p. 94.

[11] Ibid., p. 96.

Great Expecta...
Romans 15:20–2...

For several decades, Dr. Charles McCoy pastored a church in Oyster Bay, New York. While pastoring as a single man, he had time to continue his education. He eventually earned seven graduate and post-graduate degrees. When he turned seventy-two, his Baptist denomination required that he retire from ministry. Reluctantly, he stepped away from the pulpit and the people he had faithfully pastored for decades.

He was not quite sure what to do with himself. He wrote, "I keep thinking that my life's over, and I haven't really done anything yet. I've pastored this church for so many years…I've spent a lot of time working for degrees, but I haven't won very many people to the Lord."

One week after his retirement party, he met a missionary who invited him to come to India to preach. Dr. McCoy deferred, citing his age. Besides, he had never been overseas, had never traveled across America, or for that matter, flown in a plane. He could not imagine traveling to India. Not the least of his concerns was the fact that he did not have that kind of money.

The thought of going, however, nagged at him. Finally, seventy-two year old, white haired Dr. Charles McCoy announced

...eed go to India. He sold his car and a few posses-
...uy a one-way ticket to Bombay.

...s friends were horrified. They asked, "What if you fall ill?
...hat if you should die in India?"

He replied with new-found faith and courage, "It's just as close to heaven from there as it is from here."

Dr. McCoy arrived in Bombay with his billfold, his passport, a satchel of clothes, and his Bible—all of which were taken in a matter of minutes by some very clever pickpockets. He was left with only the clothes on his back and the address of the missionaries.

The man who had originally invited him to come and preach had decided to stay in America, so when he showed up on the missionaries' doorstep, they were not sure what to do with him. They invited him in and gave him a small guest room.

Dr. McCoy was anxious to do something for Christ. After two days of getting acclimated, he announced to the missionaries that he was going to visit the mayor of Bombay.

"Don't waste your time," his new friends advised. After several years of trying, they had never been able to see the mayor.

However, Dr. McCoy had prayed about it and went anyway, without an appointment. He presented his business card to the receptionist, who looked at it carefully and then, disappeared through a door. Returning, she told him to come back at 3 o'clock.

Dr. McCoy returned that afternoon to find a reception in his honor attended by some of the most important civic leaders in Bombay. It seems the city fathers had been greatly impressed by McCoy's 6'4" tall frame, his distinguished white hair, and all the degrees after his name. "He is a very important person," they thought, "perhaps even a representative of the President of the United States."

Dr. McCoy was able to speak for a half hour, giving his testimony and speaking to them about Jesus Christ. At the end, he was politely applauded by the assembled crowd. Afterward, he was approached by a man in an impressive military uniform. The man invited him to speak to the students of his military school, which—as it turned out—was India's equivalent to West Point. After his first address, McCoy was invited back repeatedly.

Invitations soon poured in from all over India, so he began an itinerant ministry of preaching the gospel. In Calcutta, he started a church for Chinese believers. He was asked to do the same in Hong Kong, where he was invited to come and live. He was then invited to Egypt and the Middle East, traveling everywhere with an energy that he had seldom felt before.

He traveled and preached, planting churches, teaching in schools, discipling believers, speaking before government leaders and dignitaries in several countries. His international ministry would last for sixteen years. He died at the age of eighty-eight, in Calcutta, India, just before he was to preach downtown at a special rally to men.

Dr. Charles McCoy never once came back to America.

Can you imagine the challenges and changes in his life? As a forty or fifty or even a seventy year old man, he had no idea what God had in mind. Had God informed him what He had up His divine sleeve for Dr. McCoy when he was in his seventy-second year, he probably would have fainted dead away.

This is like Daniel of old, whose life had a dramatic reversal and who entered the lion's den in his eighty's, although some think he was in his ninety's. What a way to go! But God had still more surprises in store.

In truth, we all have our list of expectations. Whether we have written them down or not, we have a mental list that looks something like this:

- These are three things I expect God to do with my life
- These are four things I do not expect to ever go through
- These are two things that I expect God to do with my career by the time I turn thirty or forty
- This is where I will live and this is what I want to be doing by the time I am fifty or sixty
- These are two things I expect God to do while I am in school
- These are the things I expect God to provide for my children
- These are three things I expect God will do with my finances

We all have our own original volume written in our hearts, entitled *Great Expectations*. And they might be great things indeed.

However, what if these expectations do not come true? What if God has something entirely different in mind for you? This is exactly what happened in the life of the apostle Paul.

Paul's Obsession

It is as if Paul opens up his first century Day-Timer to show us where he has penciled in certain plans. Some of it is not in pencil—it is in water resistant, permanent, magic marker.

However, before he reveals his plans, Paul reveals his passion.

And thus I aspired to preach the gospel… (Romans 15:20)

The word "aspired" does not quite carry the same punch as the original compound word Paul used. *Philotimeomai,* means, "to love and to honor."[1] Paul is saying that this is the honorable love of his heart; this is his passion; his ambition; his obsession.

Not only was Paul obsessed with godly living, the grace of God, and the glory of God, but he also had a holy obsession for the global advancement of Christ's gospel. He was obsessed with the great commission.

Ask someone what they are passionate about; what they obsess over and you will discover a great deal about that person. Paul would say, "I am obsessed with the declaration of the gospel of Christ."

He quotes in Romans 15:21, from Isaiah, broadly applying the prophet's words to the process of evangelism that began in Paul's day and will continue throughout church history until Christ returns.[2] Paul says, "I plan to be in the thick of it!"

He was like a more recent missionary to Africa named David Livingstone, who was once asked, "Where do you want to go?" He responded, "Anywhere, as long as it is forward."[3]

Livingstone was passionate about reaching Africa with the gospel of Christ. Paul was likewise obsessed with reaching his world for Christ.

Edward Gibbon, in his famous work, *The Decline and Fall of the Roman Empire*, quotes a church leader named Tertullian, who explained the rapid expansion of the gospel in the first century. Tertullian wrote, "We are but of yesterday, but we have filled every place among you—cities, islands, fortresses, towns, market-places, the very camp, tribes, companies, palace, and your senate—we have left nothing [alone] but the temples of your gods."

Harnack, the German church historian, wrote that the great mission of Christianity was accomplished by means of informal missionaries.[4]

This is a wonderful description. These are neither vocational missionaries nor formally trained missionaries, but the work for Christ is accomplished by means of these informal missionaries.

This was Paul's obsession.

Paul's Objectives

Paul reveals three personal goals in Romans 15. I am longing to come to you (vs. 23); I am going to Jerusalem (vs. 25); I will go on by way of you to Spain (vs. 24, 28).

Paul had these three major ministry plans: a short-term goal to go to the believers in Rome; an immediate goal to go to Jerusalem; and a long-range goal to go to Spain.

Paul's short-term goal to go to Rome

None of Paul's objectives; none of his plans turned out like he thought they would.

For this reason I have often been prevented from coming to you; (Romans 15:22)

In other words, "I had to mark it off my calendar time and time again."

The word translated "prevented" or "hindered" is a word that means, "to cut in." It described warfare in Paul's day, when armies often cut deep gullies into the road so that the enemy army would have to stop and fill in the ditch before they could drive their wagons across.

We talk about hitting "a bump in the road" or "an obstacle in our path," which convey the same idea.

Paul is picturing himself on a wagon, driving at full speed toward Rome, but he has to stop again and again because the road is not passable. Other things come up. Other ministries demand his attention. Other believers need help. Not to mention the beatings and hardships and shipwrecks he experiences along the way.

How long has Paul been hindered from going to Rome?

But now, with no further place for me in these regions, and since I have had for many years a longing to come to you. (Romans 15:23)

Did you catch this? Paul says, "I have been longing to come to you for many years!"

Paul would go forward in his calendar a few months and write in bold letters, "Going to Rome." Then, it would not happen. So, he would go forward another month or two and with great longing, write, "Going to Rome now." Paul did this for years.

Maybe you have longed for something good and godly for six months or for a year or for several years. Paul will long for most of his Christian life to go to Rome. Then, when he finally gets to Rome, it will be nothing like he imagined. He will not arrive in Rome as a pioneer, he will arrive as a prisoner.

If you happen to believe that a Christian has been vaccinated against misfortune, you are going to be disappointed at the first sign of sickness.

If you are under the impression that the closer a person walks with God, the more likely his plans will pan out, you are in for a big surprise.

If you believe that obeying the Lord guarantees a life without interruption and disruption, you had better buckle up because you are in for the ride of your life.

You may never *have* so much trouble; you may never *be in* so much trouble; you may never *create* so much trouble as you will when you live with an obsession to advance the name and glory and gospel of Jesus Christ.

Paul longed to go to Rome. Why? For one thing, it was the capital city of the Roman Empire.

I have the privilege of going to the Capitol Building in Raleigh to preach to an assembly of pastors and political leaders on the topic of the importance of preaching the Word of God in bringing about social reformation. As thrilled as I am about this opportunity to speak, along with three other Christian leaders, I cannot imagine how Paul must have longed to preach the gospel in the palace of Caesar; to deliver the Word to the Roman senators and philosophers—to the movers and shakers of his world.

Even more, Paul wanted to help the Roman believers grow.

I do not want you to be unaware, brethren, that often I have planned to come to you (and have been prevented so far) so that I may obtain some fruit among you... *(Romans 1:13)*

In other words, "I want to be a part of your spiritual growth. I want the joy of growing with you."

So Paul wants to go to Rome because of its influence in the empire; because of his influence on the believers, and because of their potential influence on him.

Whenever I go to Spain—for I hope to see you in passing, and to be helped on my way there by you,... *(Romans 15:24)*

The words "helped on my way" are from the verb *propempo*, which refers to helping someone on their journey by providing food and money, even companions to travel along if they can, perhaps even providing the means of travel.[5]

Paul is openly asking for food and money. This is, in a very real sense, a missionary support letter.

Those who have gone on short term missions trips know what this is all about. You get out your family phone directory and write to all your aunts and uncles and nieces and nephews; you write to your former church, your teachers, and every friend you think you have, and even some you have not been friendly with for years. As you write, you pray. As you put the letters in the mailbox, you pray. As you wait to hear back, you pray.

Paul is writing to the Romans, "I need your financial support." He was no doubt praying for years for the support he would need to make it to Spain.

Paul was adopting the same strategy that you have probably seen with missionaries and ministries and have perhaps, adopted yourselves as you raised money for your own missions trips.

This is the strategy that I remember reading about years ago, written very succinctly by Adoniram Judson. This great missionary to Burma in the mid 1800s said, "When it comes to the matter of raising funds for the work of the ministry, I ask God…and I tell the people of God."

What great advice. You tell the people, but you are ultimately, depending upon God.

Paul's immediate goal to go to Jerusalem

But now, I am going to Jerusalem serving the saints. For Macedonia and Achaia have been pleased to make a contribution for the poor among the saints in Jerusalem. Yes, they were pleased to do so, and they are indebted to them. For if the Gentiles have shared in their spiritual things, they are indebted to minister to them also in material things. (Romans 15:25–27)

When Paul wrote this letter to the Romans, the church in Jerusalem was suffering not only great persecution, but great poverty. There was a famine throughout Palestine and, because of persecution by unbelieving Jews, many Christians had lost their jobs and many others had been put in prison, which made bad conditions even worse for their families.

In addition, many foreign Jews who were visiting Jerusalem for the Feast of Pentecost were converted to Christ and decided to remain in the city and become a part of the Jerusalem church. They became house guests of believers who lived there, adding to the overall state of emergency.[6]

I love Paul's inspired choice of words when he refers to this contribution he was taking to the church in Jerusalem (verse 26). He uses the Greek word *koinonia*, which is often translated "fellowship." This is a great choice of words because this offering really was more than money; more than nickels and dimes. It was a relationship; it was fellowship; it was the sharing of life.

One of the reasons Paul was so passionate about taking this offering to the Jews was that it had been given by Gentiles. In this era of prejudice, when the race issue of Jew and Gentile was yet to be overcome, this offering was incredibly significant. The Gentile believers were clearly saying, "We are related to you. This is an expression of our communion and fellowship with you."

It was a magnificent testimony to the equality of the Christians. It was also a magnificent testimony to the unity of the church.

Paul wanted to make sure everyone got the message: we are not just members of isolated congregations—we are members of the church worldwide.[7]

For those who are preparing to travel on a missions trip—you will discover that no matter where you go in the world, when you meet other believers in other states or on different continents, there will be an immediate kinship; there will be the basis for an immediate fellowship.

> *Therefore, when I have finished this, and have put my seal on this fruit of theirs… (Romans 15:28)*

The word for seal indicates a sealing for the sake of integrity. A papyrus fragment from Paul's day, speaks of "sealing sacks of grain in order to guarantee their contents."[8] Paul wanted to make sure all the money arrived safely to the Jerusalem church.

Paul's long-term goal to go to Spain

> *…I will go on by way of you to Spain. (Romans 15:28)*

If you could have interviewed Paul, you might have asked, "Paul, what do you believe God wants you to do in the next five years?"

He would have said, "Take this offering to Jerusalem, spend time in Rome building up the believers, and then pioneer the gospel in Spain."

Why did Paul want to pioneer the gospel in Spain? Because Spain was producing the great minds of his generation. Seneca, the prime minister of the empire of Rome, was a Spaniard; Quintilian, the master of Roman oratory, was from Spain;

Lucan, the poet, was a Spaniard. Perhaps Paul was thinking that he wanted to influence the leaders of the next generation.

More than likely, Paul wanted to go to Spain because Spain was considered to be the end of the civilized world. Paul wanted to take the gospel, as Christ commanded, to the ends of the earth.

Paul said, "I'm going to Spain!"

This was the region Jonah had tried to escape to centuries earlier. Spain included the city of Tarshish. Jonah never made it to Spain either. He was given a free ride to Nineveh and a fish story people still cannot believe.

This was the region from which Solomon brought shipments of gold, silver, ivory, apes, and peacocks (1 Kings 10:22).

These are Paul's plans, but he will never make it to Spain. He will make it to Jerusalem. The book of Acts records Paul's journey in which he delivers the money to the needy community of believers.

- Acts 21 records the shocking development that a week after arriving, Jews from Asia stir up the crowds in Jerusalem against Paul. Roman soldiers intervene and prevent him from being murdered, but place him under arrest.

- Acts 22 reveals that on the next day, Paul stands trial before the Jewish Sanhedrin—the Jewish Supreme Court—and is condemned to death. The Roman soldiers again intervene and rescue him from being killed, but keep him in custody.

- Acts 23 through 26 informs us that Paul is transferred to Caesarea where he remains in prison for two years. He appeals to give his testimony to Nero and is granted his appeal.

- Acts 27 informs us that Paul, under guard, finally sets sail for Rome and—wouldn't you know it—his ship is torn apart at sea by a fierce storm and they are shipwrecked on the island of Malta. They end up spending the winter on Malta.

- Acts 28 tells us they finally make it to Rome where Paul is placed under house arrest. He is able to meet with Roman Christians—all who would come to his apartment. After two years, it seems that he was released for a time, but then arrested again and ultimately, martyred by the Roman emperor Nero.[9]

Paul never made it to Spain. His long term goal was never realized.

As for his short term goal, he made it to Rome, but Paul will not be able to personally build the church, for he will come bound in chains. Paul will not experience the life of a missionary, he will experience the death of a martyr. At the time when Paul writes Romans chapter 15, he did not know this yet. We do.

Paul's great expectations were not fulfilled. His prayers in this regard were not answered like he had hoped; his longings were never fulfilled like he had expected.

Observations about Great Expectations

Your life may seem to be held up or slowed down during times you expected it to take off.

Why are there delays? Why is the road torn up so you cannot drive your wagon across and keep on going? "Let's go, Lord! Let's get to Rome."

God never fully explained it to Paul, until after he arrived home. Someone once wrote, "The Lord orders the steps of a good man and He orders his stops as well." When we say we believe God is sovereign, we are saying that we believe God does not owe us an explanation for the steps or the stops.

Your life may involve experiences and challenges you never expected to face.

Who would have expected a riot, a trial, a shipwreck, a house arrest? Perhaps Paul was tempted to think, "Lord, how does this make any sense? How am I to endure years of house arrest and hindrances to the full expression of my heart's desire to preach to the ends of the earth?"

As with Paul, God will often not clarify what we can endure until we are in the middle of it!

Sustaining grace is never measured out ahead of time. It is measured out day by day, for His mercies are new every morning.

Once Paul was in the middle of it, his outlook had dramatically changed from that of Romans 15. Paul would write to Timothy, while under house arrest,

...do not be ashamed...of me His prisoner; but join with me in suffering for the gospel according to the power of God...I am not ashamed; for I know whom I have believed and I am convinced that He is able to guard what I have entrusted to Him until that day. (2 Timothy 1:8, 12)

> **Your life may turn in a direction**
> **you never expected to journey.**

One thing that Paul thought would happen to him, did happen.

I know that when I come to you, I will come in the fullness of the blessing of Christ. (Romans 15:29)

Do not ever believe that the fullness of Christ's blessing means you are without chains or difficulties or challenges. Do not make the mistake of believing that God's blessing is always smooth sailing; always without ruts in the road. The exact opposite could be true!

When Paul came to Rome, he was in the fullness of Christ's blessing.

Observations about God's Sovereign Plan

God does not always defend His decisions (if at all), but He asks that we surrender to Him anyway. God does not always provide answers for life's interruptions, but He asks that we trust Him in spite of them. God does not always explain His unexpected plans, but He asks that we rely upon Him as we go through them.

Our problem is that we most often say to God, "Oh Lord, I don't understand. These aren't the plans I've made for You. I know the plans I have for You!"

We need to stop telling God what to do and instead *listen* to Him. God says, "I know the plans I have for you. I have plans for you and they will ultimately give you a future and a hope."

When our great expectations are not met, He remains great! We must learn that He is our greatest expectation.

Did you know that Christ Himself became the great expectation of Paul? It was no longer traveling to Spain or preaching in Rome.

Paul would write to Timothy, near the end of his life,

...until the appearing of our Lord Jesus Christ, which He will bring about at the proper time—He who is the blessed and only Sovereign, the King of kings and Lord of lords, who alone possesses immortality and dwells in unapproachable light...To Him be honor and eternal dominion! Amen. (1 Timothy 6:15-16)

---

[1] Fritz Rienecker and Cleon Rogers, *Linguistic Key to the Greek New Testament* (Regency, 1976), p. 382.

[2] John MacArthur, *Romans: Volume 2* (Moody Press, 1994), p. 337.

[3] William Barclay, *Romans* (Westminster Press, 1955), p. 203.

[4] James Montgomery Boice, *Romans: Volume 4*, (Baker Books, 1995), p. 1875.

[5] Rienecker and Rogers, p. 383.

[6] MacArthur, p. 346.

[7] Barclay, p. 205.

[8] *Zondervan Illustrated Bible Backgrounds Commentary* (Zondervan, 2002), p. 90.

[9] Kenneth Boa and William Kruidenier, *Holman New Testament Commentary: Romans* (Holman, 2000), p. 455.

On Your Mark, Get Set...Pray!
Romans 15:30–33

S teve May recorded an interesting story in one of his books about a young boy named Gilbert. When he was eight years old, Gilbert joined the Cub Scouts. He had only been a member for a short time when, during one of his first meetings, he was handed a sheet of instructions, a block of pine wood, and four little tires. He was told to take all of this home and give it to his dad.

This was not an easy task for Gilbert, since there was no dad at home. So the block of wood remained untouched for weeks. Finally, his mother stepped in to help figure it out and the project began. Having no carpentry skills, she simply read and explained the directions to Gilbert and let him do all the work—which he did happily. They read the measurements, the rules of what could and could not be done, and within a few days, his block of pine wood turned into a "pinewood derby car." It was a little lopsided, but it looked okay to them, and they proudly named it "Blue Lightning."

Finally, the big night arrived. With Blue Lightning in his hand and excitement bursting in his heart, Gilbert and his mom headed to the race. Once there, it was obvious that Gilbert's car was the only one made entirely by a Cub Scout.

All the other cars had slick paint jobs and sleek body styles designed for speed. Some of the other boys laughed when they saw his crude little lopsided car.

Gilbert was undeterred and waited his turn. The race was a process of elimination—a car was kept in the race as long as it was a winner. And Blue Lightning kept winning. In the final run, it was Blue Lightning against the sleekest, fasted looking car Gilbert had seen that night. Just as the final race was about to begin, Gilbert asked if he could pray. The race stopped. With a wrinkled brow and a hand clutching his little derby car, Gilbert bowed his head for a very long minute and prayed to his Heavenly Father. Then he announced, "I'm ready now."

The crowd cheered with anticipation. Gilbert watched his block of wood swoosh down the ramp with surprising speed and cross the finish line a fraction of a second in front of the other car. Gilbert jumped into the air and shouted, "Thank You!" as the crowd roared in approval.

The Scout Master, with microphone in hand, asked Gilbert, "So, you prayed to be the winner, huh, Gilbert?"

To this, Gilbert responded with a surprising answer, "Oh, no sir, that wouldn't be fair. I just asked God to help me so I wouldn't cry when I lost."[1]

I wonder how much of our praying is motivated by a desire for winning in life, rather than responding to life. I wonder how much of the believer's prayer life is directed to life working out, rather than how to act when it does not.

If the Christian life could be analogous to a Pinewood Derby, we would all look a lot like Blue Lightning. There is no

Christian alive who is not like Gilbert's car—a little lopsided; a little rough around the edges; unevenly painted; anything but sleek and impressive. The body of Christ is not made up of engineering perfections, but blocks of common pine in need of shaping, molding, and refining.

Frankly, we need to pray more, not to come in first, but how to race with a Christ-like spirit regardless of what place we come in.

If ever there was a sleek model of Christianity—spiritually aerodynamic, and perfectly balanced—it was the apostle Paul. If anyone knew how to win, it was this converted Jewish attorney who became the pioneer missionary for the cause of Christ.

Yet, over and over again, the apostle Paul begged the church to pray for him as he began a new lap in his race. Paul asked the Ephesians for prayer that he might be able to speak boldly for the sake of,

...the gospel, for which I am an ambassador in chains... and pray on my behalf, that...I may speak boldly, as I ought to speak. (Ephesians 6:19, 20)

He begged the Corinthians to be,

...joining in helping [me] through your prayers...(2 Corinthians 1:11)

He implored the Thessalonians, concerning the entire missionary team, to

...pray for us that the word of the Lord will spread rapidly...and that we will be rescued from...evil men [who seek to do us harm]. (2 Thessalonians 3:1–2)

He encouraged the Philippians to remember that their prayers for him would be,

...the reason for my [effectiveness]...(Philippians 1:19)

He reminded the Colossians to be,

...praying...that God will open...a door for [me in the ministry]. (Colossians 4:3)

You might think that Paul would see doors open automatically; that sermons and speeches would flow effortlessly from his lips; that he would never shrink back in fear, but would naturally speak with boldness. However, over and over again, Paul stood beside the race track of life with his little blue car, about to hear the race master say, "On your mark, get set..." and Paul would say, "Wait! Can we pray?"

Why? Is Paul praying so that things will work out? Sure, but more than that, Paul is praying in case things do not work out. Paul was obsessed with prayer for God's will to be accomplished in his life—no matter what it was.

Paul's Obsession with Prayer

Now I urge you, brethren, by our Lord Jesus Christ and by the love of the Spirit, to strive together with me in your prayers to God for me. (Romans 15:30)

We get the idea that Paul does not view himself as a spiritual "Lone Ranger." He is part of the body of Christ and is asking for the body's help. This letter to the Romans was, among many other things, a missionary letter, in which Paul is asking for support. Earlier, Paul asks "...to be helped on my way..." (Romans 15:24). This is a word for financial assistance; for food.

Now, as in any good missionary letter, Paul asks for prayer. However, he does not just ask! His words are packed with intense vocabulary. The words "I urge you" could be translated from *parakalo*, meaning, "I beg you; I exhort you." Donald Grey Barnhouse said, "This word carries the urgency of an SOS"[2]—I am calling you to pray for me.

However, remember the prayer is not just on Paul's account, but is ultimately for the namesake of,

> *...our Lord Jesus Christ and by the love of the [Holy] Spirit... (Romans 15:30)*

In other words, Paul is asking for prayer, but reminding the believers that true prayer ultimately seeks the glory of Jesus Christ and obeys the unifying call of the Holy Spirit to love one another.

Paul wants people to join him who want to see Christ honored and the Spirit of God demonstrated through the love of the body for Christ.

"I urge you," or "I summon you; I beg you." This is the same verb Paul used earlier in his letter,

> *Therefore I urge you, brethren, by the mercies of God, to present your bodies a living and holy sacrifice, acceptable to God, which is your spiritual service of worship. (Romans 12:1)*

How important is it for believers to give their lives to God? It is really not optional, is it?

Paul employs the same verb as if to say, "It cannot be an option that you pray for me, for the glory of Christ and the love of the Spirit."

However, Paul goes even further saying,

...strive together with me in your prayers to God for me, (Romans 15:30)

I will not bore you with all the details, but I can remember being in the delivery room with Marsha when we were about to have our fourth child. I say "we" rather generously. If it were up to men to have babies, the world would have none—not one— ever! We would not be able to take the incredible pain, not to mention the physical demands and emotional strain of carry- ing and then delivering a baby. Forget it! We could never do it!

I will never forget the intensity of my wife's pain in the delivery room on that Halloween night nearly thirteen years ago. She gripped my arm—that would never be the same again—and looked up with her blue eyes filled with a mixture of pain and fear, and said, "Help me." I have never felt more helpless in the face of my wife's utter agony.

This is the word Paul uses in this verse, translated, "strive together with me." It is the word, *sunagonizomai*, from which we get our word, "agony." He is literally saying, "agonize with me."

This is the only time this compound word is found in the entire New Testament, though other derivatives are used. For instance, when Christ said,

...My kingdom is not of this world. If My kingdom were of this world, then My servants would be fighting...(John 18:36)

Paul used a shorter derivative of this word when he said,

I have fought the good fight...(2 Timothy 4:7)

Paul is not asking the believer to say a couple of short prayers on his behalf, with words like, "Well, Lord, please bless Paul out there somewhere...Amen."

This is the same word used of Jesus Christ when He prayed in the Garden of Gethsemane,

And being in agony He was praying very fervently; and His sweat became like drops of blood, falling down upon the ground. (Luke 22:44)

Imagine that—Paul is asking the Romans to agonize with him like Christ agonized before the Father.

This is not the kind of prayer that is limited to an hour-long prayer meeting at church. This obsession is not restricted to the bulletin or the prayer sheet or the online prayer list.

This is spiritual labor. This is entering the contest of life and every time you hear the game keeper say, "On your mark, get set..." you want to say, "Wait...not until I've prayed." I will confess to you that I usually get passionate about praying only after Blue Lightning is in fourth gear.

Frankly, I think this kind of obsession for intercession is what Paul had in mind when he wrote to the Thessalonian believers to,

pray without ceasing; (1 Thessalonians 5:17)

R. A. Torrey once wrote ten reasons that we should pray like Paul exhorts us to pray. We should pray in this way because:

- There is a devil and prayer is the God appointed means of resisting him.
- Prayer is God's way for us to obtain what we need from Him.
- The apostles considered prayer to be the priority business in their lives.
- Prayer occupied a prominent place and played a very important part in the earthly life of our Lord.
- Prayer is the present ministry of our Lord, since He is now interceding for us.
- Prayer is the means God has appointed for our receiving mercy from Him and help in time of need.
- Prayer is the means of obtaining the fullness of God's joy.
- Prayer with thanksgiving is the means of obtaining freedom from anxiety and peace which passes understanding.
- Prayer is the means by which we are to keep watchful and be alert.
- Prayer is used by God to promote our spiritual growth, bring power into our work, lead others to faith in Christ, and bring all other blessings to Christ's church.

After reading a list like this, the question is not, "Should we pray?" but, "How can we afford not to?"

I wonder if Reuben Torrey was especially passionate about prayer because of his own story. He never forgot that one night as an unbelieving student at Yale, overwhelmed with grief and guilt over his sinful lifestyle, he decided to take his own life.

That night, in 1875, he stumbled to the wash basin in his dormitory room, looking for his razor to cut his wrists, in such guilt over his rebellious life, having rejected the gospel of his mother and father. He could not find his razor and suddenly became overwhelmed with conviction to pray. Unknown to him, his mother, at that very hour, was inwardly compelled to get on her knees and begin praying for the salvation of her son many miles away. At the same hour, Reuben knelt by his bed and gave his life to Jesus Christ.

R. A. Torrey went on to become the president of Moody Bible Institute. He would remain passionate about prayer his entire life.

Paul's Specific Prayer Requests

Now, as any good missionary letter will model, Paul becomes extremely specific in this urgent matter of prayer. In fact, he will deliver three specific prayer requests for the church in Rome to pray over.

Safety

That I may be rescued from those who are disobedient in Judea,... (Romans 15:31a)

Paul was "enemy #1" of the Jewish people. His face was plastered on bulletin boards in every post office in Jerusalem.

The Jews in Jerusalem had already killed Stephen after he delivered his first and only sermon. They had thrown Peter in prison, only to have lost him in a miraculous escape as an angel came and delivered him. The blood of the Christians had already stained the soil in and around the city.

Paul, the former prosecutor of Christianity, is now the famous preacher of Christianity. The Jews are infuriated at his conversion to Christ and his doctrines of this new thing called the church.

Paul fully understood that he was headed for trouble. He was, in fact, walking into the path of a tornado. In this verse, Paul says, "Agonize with me that I might be rescued from the unbelieving Jews." His word translated "rescue" or "deliver" (*rhuomai*) is a word that means, "to be preserved."

Our Lord used this word as He taught us to pray to be delivered from the lure of the evil one,

...deliver us from evil. (Matthew 6:13)

It is also used to describe the redemption of believers who are,

...rescued from the domain of darkness, and trans-ferred...to the kingdom of His beloved Son, (Colossians 1:13)

Paul knew that he was a wanted man and that unless the Lord protected him, he would die in Jerusalem.

The evidence of the Jews' hatred for Paul was seen in the events that occurred soon after Paul arrived in Jerusalem. According to Acts 21, Paul is indeed recognized by some Jews as he goes to the temple. His enemies see him and stir up the masses of the people, shouting,

"Men of Israel, come to our aid! This is the man who preaches to all men everywhere against our people and the Law and this place; and besides he has even brought Greeks into the temple and has defiled this holy place."... and all the city was provoked, and the people rushed together, and taking hold of Paul, they dragged him out of the temple and...[began to beat him]. (Acts 21:28–32)

Can you imagine this riot that breaks out? Paul will nearly be beaten to death by this mob who want to pay him back for betraying Judaism and for openly declaring that Jesus was the Messiah. They would have killed him had the Roman soldiers not rescued him from this mob.

So Paul's first prayer request for safety was answered— although not exactly the way Paul expected. And probably not the way the Roman believers had prayed.

We would expect God to answer our prayers for safety in a way that does not involve getting nearly beaten to death. Safety usually does not involve near-death experiences at the hand of a bloodthirsty mob!

However, God did have Paul's protection in mind—protection by Roman soldiers, who will safely store him behind bars.

As I have thought about the assassination attempts on Paul's life, I have no doubt that he would have never survived had he remained in the care of Christians. It would require the Roman empire to defend his life.

Roman soldiers would be assigned to guard Paul for the rest of his life. Without them, I do not believe he would have had the opportunity to write his letters and guide the church with his inspired doctrine. The first prayer request was answered in an unusual manner.

Perhaps God is answering your prayers, but in a way you would not have chosen or even thought of. You would never have scripted an answer in the way it played out, but after time and growth and insight, through the tears and travail, you are beginning to understand.

Perhaps you have just begun to know what this kind of agonizing prayer is all about.

I once heard a humorous story told about three friends who were discussing the proper posture for prayer.

The first one said, "Christians ought to be on their knees with their heads bowed in reverence to God."

The second friend replied, "No, Christians should stand with their head raised, looking into the heavens, and speaking into the face of God."

The third spoke up, "I know nothing about that, but I do know this: the finest praying I've ever done was upside down in a well that I'd fallen into!"

Suddenly, the meaning of "to agonize in prayer" dawned on this third man, and it did not matter if his eyes were open or closed—he did his finest praying upside down in a well.

Paul's second prayer request is equally, if not more, significant to the cause of Christ and the love of the Holy Spirit than his first.

Service

*And that my service for Jerusalem may prove acceptable
to the saints; (Romans 15:31b)*

Remember that the relationship between the Jew and the Gentile was abominable. Throughout the ministry of Paul, there were Jews who never came around—they argued with Paul and debated his insistence that Gentiles did not have to become Jews to enter the church.

So Paul had unbelieving Jews who wanted to kill him and believing Jews who would be cool toward him. Paul was hoping that the offering he was delivering to the church in Jerusalem would help heal the rift and encourage the unity of love in the Spirit.

Would the Jews be offended? Would they think the Gentiles were being superior in their gifts? Would they think the Gentiles were trying to buy their affections? All of these were possibilities.

So much of this is lost on us because of time and distance and culture. Imagine what it was like.

The temple of Paul's day had been built by Herod the Great. Much of it was overlaid with gold. It sat on a raised earth platform, known as the temple mount, and was surrounded by courts. The innermost court was called the Court of the Priests because only members of the priestly tribe of Levi were permitted to enter. The next court further out was the Court of Israel and could be entered by any Jewish male. The court beyond this was the Court of the Women which could be entered by any Jewish woman or any Jewish person for that matter.

Now note this: although there were differences, these three courtyards were all on the same level. However, this changed past the Court of Women. One had to descend five steps to a level area where a five-foot stone wall was built that went around the entire temple. Gates were installed through which the Jewish people could take stairs up to the Courts of Women and Men and Priests, but no Gentiles were allowed.

From this level ground, where the stone wall was built, one had to descend fourteen more steps to another level space, called the Court of the Gentiles. Nineteen steps below the Jewish courts, and on that stone wall, there were inscriptions warning the Gentiles. One was unearthed in 1871, which read, "No foreigner is to enter within the wall and embankment around the sanctuary. Whoever is caught will have himself to blame for his death which follows."[3]

The signs were clear, "Gentile trespassers will be killed."

It is no wonder that the orthodox Jewish man would rise every morning and thank God that he had not been born a Gentile.

Now, this Jewish man comes to faith in Christ. Now he discovers that the ground at the foot of the cross is level. There are no steps in the church that separate Jew and Gentile. Jew and Gentile alike have been born into a new race,

...a chosen race,...a holy nation, a people of God's own possession, so that [they] may proclaim the excellencies

of Him who has called [them] out of darkness into His marvelous light; (1 Peter 2:9)

It was all so new—grace was intimidating; the gospel was humbling. Would they accept Paul's gift of money, collected primarily from Gentile churches?

This is the reason Paul asks the Roman believers to,

...[pray] that my service for Jerusalem may prove acceptable to the saints; (Romans 15:31b)

This prayer request was answered exactly as Paul had hoped! Luke records the event in Acts.

After we arrived in Jerusalem, the brethren received us gladly...After [Paul] had greeted them, he began to relate one by one the things which God had done among the Gentiles. And when they heard it they began glorifying God. (Acts 21:17–20)

Paul's service to the saints was acceptable. Praise God!

Spirit

So that I may come to you in joy by the will of God and find refreshing rest in your company. (Romans 15:32)

In a tender and open manner, Paul refers to the Roman church as a safe harbor he cannot wait to sail into. One author said,

"Paul desperately wanted to drop anchor in the quiet haven of the assembly in Rome and rest. He had left Ephesus in an uproar; he had conflicted with Corinth over their immaturity and sin; he had written sharp words to the Galatian churches…he just wanted to rest—to spend time refreshing his spirit and recharge his batteries with joy…that was the longing of his soul."[4]

Paul would be arrested in Jerusalem, and several years later arrive in Rome—not the pioneering missionary, but the prisoner who will one day become a martyr for Christ.

How did the church in Rome receive him? I wish I could tell a different story, but we know that when he first arrived in Rome, only a few believers came to meet him. The rest of the believers were afraid to make themselves known because of the chains and the Roman guards and the potential of persecution.[5]

In his final letter to Timothy, Paul wrote of the Roman believer's fear and timidity, if not cowardice.

You are aware that all…turned away from me…The Lord grant mercy to the house of Onesiphorus, for he often refreshed me and was not ashamed of my chains; but when he was in Rome, he eagerly searched for me and found me—the Lord grant to him to find mercy from the Lord…(2 Timothy 1:15–18)

So Paul was refreshed after all. Not by the assembly, but by one family who came and visited him—risking their own safety.

Did Paul lack joy? No. That prayer request was answered.

It would be in Rome, under house arrest, that Paul would write his letter to the Philippians—a letter drenched with joy. In fact, the word *joy* will appear sixteen times in this letter.

Paul had discovered God's will was vastly different than his earlier prayer list. He was willing to allow God's spirit to change his spirit, so that, even in the face of dramatic reversals, Paul would come to Rome and find joy.

Paul's Amen

Now the God of peace be with you all. Amen. (Romans 15:33)

Paul ends this paragraph with a customary Jewish benediction, in which he references the peace of God that would be able to blend Jew and Gentile into one harmonious body.

Spiritual maturity does not automatically erase the pain of an unsettled heart.

Paul was facing danger, battle, hatred, prejudice, conflict, and possibly death. Such unsettled feelings brought an agony that he needed to share. He needed others to pray—yes, pray for the great apostle Paul.

We are most often tempted to use prayer for God to change our circumstances, when God is using circumstances to change us.

A disciplined prayer life does not automatically erase the potential of unanswered questions.

Intimacy with God does not alleviate times of wondering and confusion and even discouragement.

Walking with God does not always mean your Blue Lightning Pinewood Derby car comes in first place—sometimes it comes in last. You cannot figure out the reason; and God chooses not to give you answers.

An obsession with intercession is surrendering to a sovereign God who has the right to answer in any way He pleases—even if He chooses not to answer at all.

E. Stanley Jones wrote,

> Prayer is simply surrender to God. If I throw out a boat hook from a boat and catch hold of the shore and pull, do I pull the shore to me, or do I pull myself to the shore? Prayer is not pulling God to my will, but the aligning of my will to whatever God wants.[6]

A commitment to serve Christ does not automatically erase the possibility of an uncertain future.

In a very touching scene as the apostle Paul was about to set sail for Jerusalem, he bade farewell to the elders of the Ephesian church. In his comments, he made this remarkable statement,

> *...I am on my way to Jerusalem, not knowing what will happen to me there, (Acts 20:22)*

Imagine that! Imagine running a race not knowing when or where the finish line will be. On your mark, get set...wait! Let us make sure we pray before, during, and after the race.

Then we can say with Paul, "Now the God of peace be with you all, Amen."

> *Peace! Perfect Peace!*
> *Our future is unknown?*
> *But Jesus Christ we know, and He is on the throne!*[7]

---

[1] Steve May, *The Story File* (Hendrickson Publishers, 2000), p. 243.

[2] Donald Grey Barnhouse, *Romans: Volume 4* (Eerdmans, 1964), p. 108.

[3] James Boice, *Romans: Volume 4* (Baker, 1995), p. 1905.

[4] R. C. H. Lenski, *The Interpretation of Romans* (Augsburg Publishing, 1936), p. 896.

[5] Barnhouse, p. 110.

[6] Charles Swindoll, *The Tale of the Tardy Oxcart* (Word Publishing, 1998), p. 453.

[7] John Phillips, *Exploring Romans* (Moody Press, 1969), p. 260.